ideals ®
EASTER

Again the ancient miracle,
As new as though it had not been!
Blossom by blossom, bell by bell,
The south winds usher Easter in.

On every hill beneath the skies,
Where winter storms have worked their strife,
April, that shining angel, cries
The resurrection and the life.

Nancy Byrd Turner

From *The Easter Book of Legends and Stories*, copyright © 1947 by Lothrop, Lee & Shepard Company, New York, NY. Excerpted by arrangement with Lothrop, Lee & Shepard, a Division of William Morrow & Co., Inc.

ISBN 0-8249-1050-8

Publisher, Patricia A. Pingry
Editor, Ramona Richards
Art Director, David Lenz
Permissions, Kathleen Gilbert
Copy Editor, Peggy Schaefer
Phototypesetter, Karen Davidson
Production Manager, Jan Johnson

IDEALS—Vol. 44, No. 2 March MCMLXXXVII IDEALS (ISSN 0019-137X) is published eight times a year,
February, March, May, June, August, September, November, December
by IDEALS PUBLISHING CORPORATION, Nelson Place at Elm Hill Pike, Nashville, Tenn. 37214-8000
Second class postage paid at Nashville, Tennessee, and additional mailing offices.
Copyright © MCMLXXXVII by IDEALS PUBLISHING CORPORATION.
POSTMASTER: Send address changes to Ideals, Post Office Box 148000, Nashville, Tenn. 37214-8000
All rights reserved. Title IDEALS registered U.S. Patent Office.
Published simultaneously in Canada.

SINGLE ISSUE—$3.50
ONE-YEAR SUBSCRIPTION—eight consecutive issues as published—$15.95
TWO-YEAR SUBSCRIPTION—sixteen consecutive issues as published—$27.95
Outside U.S.A., add $4.00 per subscription year for postage and handling.

The cover and entire contents of IDEALS are fully protected by copyright and must
not be reproduced in any manner whatsoever. Printed and bound in U.S.A.
by the Banta Co., Menasha, Wisconsin.

Front and back cover from H. Armstrong Roberts

Inside front cover by Fred Sieb

Inside back cover by Ed Cooper

March Snow

This isn't just a winter snow;
It's much too soft and warm.
Without the cold and freezing air,
It hath a springlike charm.
'Tis almost gentle on my cheek
As though it tried to say,
Do let me have this little time
For soon I'll melt away.

This isn't January snow—
For see, it's much too wet,
And certainly might prove to be
The very last we'll get.
The flakes are twirling in the air
As though they've surely found
Their beauty quickly fades from sight
When'ere they reach the ground.

This isn't really winter snow;
It's part of early spring,
A fond farewell to wintertime
Before the birds shall sing.
So very gentle in its way,
It brings a thrill to you;
A March snow soft against your cheek
Says winter's almost through.

Garnett Ann Schultz

Photo Opposite
LATE SNOW
Ina Mackey

AMERICAN CROSSROADS

Editor's Note: "American Crossroads" is a regular feature of *Ideals*, presenting photographs, stories, and jokes which have been submitted by our readers, about uniquely American events or experiences. If you have a 50 to 75 word account or photograph of an unusual or interesting occurrence unique to an American lifestyle or heritage, we would like to know. Send your submission to "American Crossroads," c/o Ideals Editorial, P.O. Box 141000, Nashville, TN 37214-1000. Please send only copies of manuscripts and duplicates of photographs or slides since submissions will not be returned. We will pay $10 for each printed submission.

courtesy of the J.B. Knowles Senior Citizens Center

Remember Grandma's featherbed with layers and layers of handmade quilts? Today, even though most of us have succumbed to more modern means of keeping warm, such as electric blankets, the art of quilting is still very much alive.

Women all over the country still get together around the quilting frame to share new recipes, ideas, and, of course, stories of their children and grandchildren. The J.B. Knowles Senior Citizen Center in Nashville, Tennessee, has quilting classes every Wednesday. Women who have never quilted before are learning this wonderful art while enjoying the fellowship of others.

Quilters take much pride in their work. Each quilt is pieced together with painstakingly small stitches, then hand-quilted. They can be as intricate as the ones shown here, or an old family design passed down through several generations. The blue and white Hawaiian Quilt pictured above took over one year to complete.

In this age of advanced technology, nothing can quite compare to snuggling down under a good, warm quilt on a cold winter's night. Knowing a friend or loved one made it just for you makes it even more special. Quilting is indeed an art that young and old alike will enjoy for many years to come.

Carol Wedekind
Nashville, Tennessee

Mailboxes—they are many things to many people.

When rural free delivery first began on October 1, 1896, mailboxes were often hollowed-out logs—fastened securely in a horizontal fashion to a sturdy fence post—an old piece of tanned hide was hanging loose for a "front door" while a piece of weathered clapboard was nailed to the three-foot log's backside, protecting its precious contents from all forms of inclement weather...and even a varmint.

In 1987—91 years after 124 letters, 290 papers, 33 postal cards, and 2 packages were delivered to patrons during the first week of rural free delivery in West Virginia—mailboxes have taken on the shapes and forms and imaginations of their owners' hobbies, occupations, and fantasies. The photos on this page illustrate some of the more innovative ideas in mailbox artistry.

Joanne Kash
Holly Hill, Florida

Joanne Kash

Joanne Kash

Joanne Kash

Ramona Richards

April

'Tis the moon of the springtime, yet never a bird
In the wind-shaken elm or the maple is heard;
For green meadow grasses, wide levels of snow,
And blowing of drifts where the crocus should blow;
Where windflower and violet, amber and white,
On south-sloping brooksides should smile in the light,
O'er the cold winter beds of their late waking roots,
The frosty flake eddies, the ice crystal shoots;
And longing for light, under wind-driven heaps
Round the boles of the pine wood the ground laurel creeps,
Unkissed of the sunshine, unbaptized of showers,
With buds scarcely swelled, which should burst into flowers!
We wait for thy coming, sweet wind of the south,
For the touch of thy light wings, the kiss of thy mouth,
For the yearly evangel thou bearest from God,
Resurrection and life to the graves of the sod!

John Greenleaf Whittier

Photo Opposite, FIRST FLOWER, Ray Elliott, Jr.

Mama's Easter

The Easter Mama always told us about was the first one after her house burned down. It was the one, she said, when she finally realized what Easter was all about.

On that chilly April day Mama had climbed the gentle hill to where her home used to stand. Several months had passed before she had found the courage to make this walk. Last autumn, after the wailing sirens and flashing lights, the shouted orders and the frantic screams had ceased, her home lay in ashes and smoldering cinders. Destroyed. Gone. Dead. It still seemed like a bad dream; difficult to acknowledge, yet very real.

She was settled in her new place, had her friends and family, yet the loss still stung. Perhaps the walk to the ruined home would enable her to lance the wound, let out the grief, find a healing.

The house was leveled, except for the front steps of charred concrete. They beckoned her in—to nothing. Piles of sodden lumber, black and damp from recent spring storms, lay in crisscross confusion. Broken window glass punctuated the wreckage, glinting in the chilly sunlight. Nothing was recognizable. Nothing except the steps. She climbed them and sat down at the top, elbows on knees, chin in hands, and studied her former home. Her garden was gone. The mementos of past years were gone. The children would never come here again. The grandchildren would never share the memories this place had held. Easter somehow seemed incongruous amid all this wreckage and destruction.

As she sat there, a tatter of purple, shaken by the wind, caught her eye. How could anything have escaped the flames? Curious, she left the steps and picked her way cautiously across the jumbled boards and shards of broken glass, then knelt to retrieve the violet scrap. It wasn't cloth at all, she realized, but a tiny crocus. Carefully, Mama pulled the soggy ashes and debris away from the little plant. The bright green pointed leaves were small, but sturdy. They had somehow pressed and pushed themselves up through inches of dirt, ashes, splintered wood, and cinders then, defiantly, opened to reveal their purple blossom. Warmed by the pale spring sun, the tissue-thin petals spread apart, baring the flower's heart.

Awed, Mama touched one green leaf. She wondered how something so frail could exist in this place. Slowly, the realization came. The stubborn little crocus only appeared fragile because of the death around it. In truth, it possessed the greatest strength of all because it dared to begin again. It refused to accept annihilation.

Standing, Mama turned and studied the burned landscape again, recalling her memories. Then she raised her eyes, squinting in the sunlight. Shading her eyes with her hand, she gazed beyond her hill, into the little town below. Atop the small village chapel she could make out the silhouette of a narrow cross. It looked so frail and fragile outlined in the spring sky. She had seen it thousands of times before, but never quite this way and suddenly, the lesson of the crocus echoed in her mind. It only looked fragile. In reality it represented the greatest strength in the universe; the ultimate triumph of life over death.

Smiling slightly, Mama turned again to look at the flower in the ashes, then she raised her eyes to the cross. This was the truth of Easter, and she had found it here in this unlikely place! Easter was not merely a day for family reunions and egg hunts for the children. Nor was it just a celebration framed with the majesty of stained glass windows, stately lilies, and Handel's "Messiah." This Easter she understood, perhaps for the first time, the lesson of new life. Easter was strength springing forth from weakness, victory wrenched from defeat, the empty tomb triumphing over the grave.

That Easter Mama turned her back on the scorched rubble and walked away from the blackened ashes. She strode confidently down the hill, leaving the memories and regrets on her old front steps, walking into the future with the freshness of spring in every step.

Pamela Kennedy

Photo Opposite
CONGREGATIONAL CHURCH
WETHERSFIELD, CONNECTICUT
Freelance Photographers Guild

Springtime

Each spring I see a brilliant color
Burst forth from Mother Earth.
I learn anew that God creates
Each flower in new birth.

Each spring a fragrance fills the air,
And butterflies will hover
To carry pollen for new growth
And make a floral cover.

Each spring I hear a redbird sing
To winter day's farewell.
There's warmth and joy upon the earth
As Springtime casts her spell.

                    Laurie Wilcox

Spring

Jumping ropes and hopscotch games,
Kites a-flying high,
Girls and boys on roller skates
Merrily pass me by.

A balmy breeze with warm bright sun,
The chirping robins sing,
Crocus bursting through the earth.
Ah! These are signs of spring.

Katherine F. Jelsema
Byron Center, Michigan

Hopscotch Fun

We made a copy of the game
With tracings of white chalk,
Dividing spaces neat and square
For hopscotch on the walk.

Then standing back a little way,
We tossed a flattened rock
And hopped to bring it back from out
Each different numbered block.

Arlane and Kelly tossed and hopped
And Cheryl did the same,
But Jackie Lee made the highest score;
She had a better aim.

We had some funtime added when
The nice new mailman came—
He smiled and hopped on one leg through
Our chalk-marked hopscotch game!

Remelda Nielsen Gibson
Tooele, Utah

Reflections

March

A tattered, dirty, little boy
With grimy hands and face,
And careless feet that trample mud
About in every place.

With boisterous ways and shouting voice
And whistle high and shrill,
Who calls his dog to heel, and roams
Through valley, over hill.

And yet he has a charming grin,
His eyes are brightly blue;
And in his hand he shyly holds
Some violets for you.

May Frink Converse
Wellsville, Kansas

Flowers Down the Garden Path

Flowers down the garden path
lift their heads and gently laugh,

Looking to the rising sun
at dawn's new day just begun,

Being washed by gentle rains,
and gently moving to the strains

Of the music of the winds,
stems that move and gracefully bend.

Flowers down the garden path
lift their heads and gently laugh.

Elizabeth Dewey
Lexington, South Carolina

Editor's Note: Readers are invited to submit unpublished, original poetry, short anecdotes, and humorous reflections on life for possible publication in future *Ideals* issues. Please send copies only; manuscripts will not be returned. Writers will receive $10 for each published submission. Send materials to "Readers' Reflections," Ideals Publishing Corporation, Nelson Place at Elm Hill Pike, Nashville, Tennessee 37214.

The Piper

Piping down the valleys wild,
   Piping songs of pleasant glee,
On a cloud I saw a child;
   And he, laughing, said to me,

"Pipe a song about a lamb!"
   So I piped with merry cheer.
"Piper, pipe that song again!"
   So I piped; he wept to hear.

"Drop thy pipe, thy happy pipe;
   Sing thy songs of happy cheer!"
So I sang the same again,
   While he wept with joy to hear.

"Piper, sit thou down, and write
   In a book, that all may read!"
So he vanished from my sight,
   And I plucked a hollow reed,

And I made a rural pen,
   And I stained the water clear;
And I wrote my happy songs
   Every child may joy to hear.

                 William Blake

Photo Opposite
SPRING FLOURISH
Fred Sieb

The Garden's Alive with Easter

The garden's alive with Easter.
The flowers bloom row on row:
Daffodils, hyacinths, tulips,
And lilies as white as snow.

The garden's alive with Easter;
A fragrant joy it displays.
The face of each smiling flower
Reflects Resurrection Day.

The garden's alive with Easter.
O, may your heart's garden be, too,
That your life might bloom with beauty,
Revealing Christ's love in you.

Loise Pinkerton Fritz

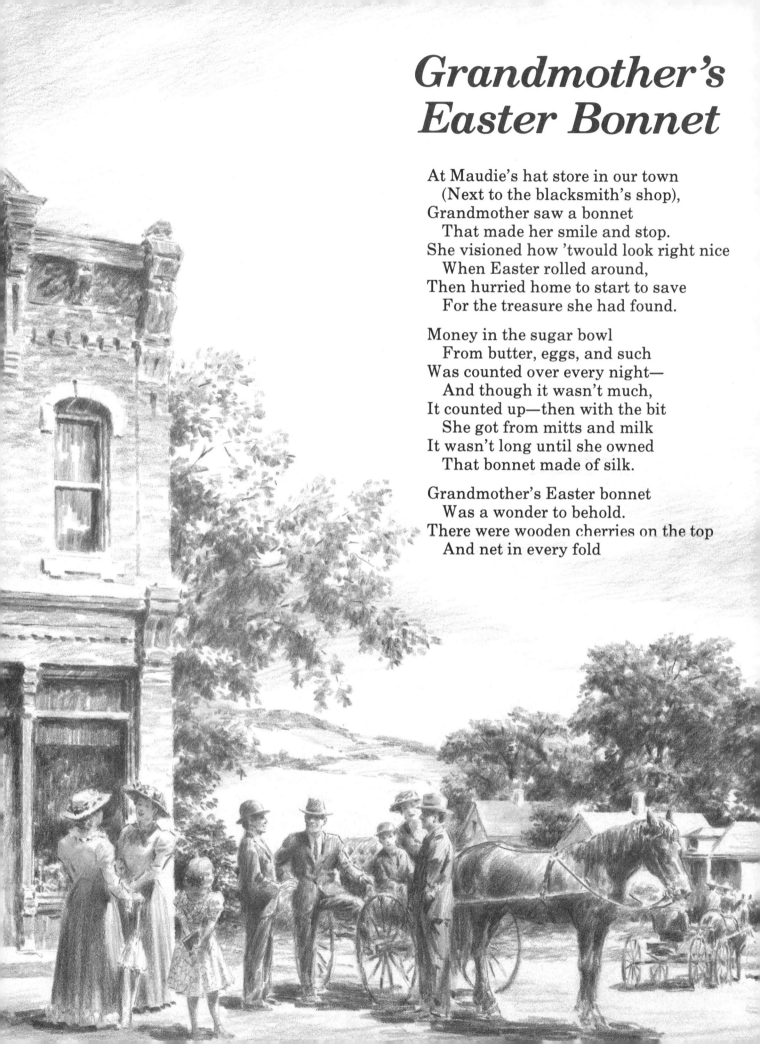

Grandmother's Easter Bonnet

At Maudie's hat store in our town
  (Next to the blacksmith's shop),
Grandmother saw a bonnet
  That made her smile and stop.
She visioned how 'twould look right nice
  When Easter rolled around,
Then hurried home to start to save
  For the treasure she had found.

Money in the sugar bowl
  From butter, eggs, and such
Was counted over every night—
  And though it wasn't much,
It counted up—then with the bit
  She got from mitts and milk
It wasn't long until she owned
  That bonnet made of silk.

Grandmother's Easter bonnet
  Was a wonder to behold.
There were wooden cherries on the top
  And net in every fold

Around the brim, and flowers
　　Nestled gently on the side.
Grandmother's Easter bonnet
　　Was the best we ever spied.

Her gray hair seemed as silver
　　Beneath its store-bought grace;
Her blue eyes sparkled with a light
　　That brightened all her face.
Pa held his breath and whistled
　　At the magic that it shed;
He said it perked her up a mite—
　　With nature on her head.

And so, off to the meetinghouse,
　　Grandfather by her side,
Grandmother walked with elegance
　　As when she was a bride.
And all the people nodded
　　As Grandmother knelt to pray
And thank the heavenly Father
　　For a lovely Easter day.

Hannah Moor

Chasing Shadows

Did you ever chase a shadow
Down a green and windy hill,
Catching shade with bare feet drumming
As the sun pushed it at will?

And the cloud that made the shadow
In the clean, cool, rain-washed sky
Raced you out across the meadow—
You thought that you would fly.

Oh, that wild exhilaration
Stays with you as you grow.
When you see soft cloud shadows,
You'll remember running long ago

Down a springtime hill in childhood
As a truant cloud played tag,
How wet grass caressed your toes,
Birds invited you to lag.

You'll remember fragrant flowers,
Breeze-filled cadences of spring,
And the brimming-over laughter
That a shadow race can bring.

Frolicsome, gay, magic shadows
Skip down April's greening hill:
Though your feet no longer chase them,
In your heart you race them still.

Nellie Gardner Condon

Bright April

This is the first bright April she has known.
She toddles through the soft, greening grass.
She pokes at willow twigs, an old pine cone...
She pours the day out through a minute glass.

Who but a tot, a year or maybe less,
Would try the flavor of a crocus bud,
Would probe the wind or see bright loveliness
In pools of stagnant water, thick with mud?

She coos duets with strands on cross-armed poles
And chuckles with the rain in dripping spouts.
She reaches hungry arms for orioles,
Sees mystery in blue jay roustabouts.

This April day with all its warmth and joy
She handles like a new and shining toy.

Helen Virden

A Boy and Springtime

I like the very best of all
The fun I have in spring.
The showers leave the puddles full.
I sail my boat with string.

It's warm enough to pitch a tent
Somewhere out on the lawn.
It takes a lot of courage
To sleep there till it's dawn.

I gather flowers in the marsh
For Mother's empty vase
And challenge Mongrel, my old dog,
To a short and heated race.

I've noticed that when springtime comes,
I fall asleep much better.
I'm really not the least bit tired,
It's just the springtime weather!

Christel B. Ellis

Spring Luncheon

Gingered Chicken with Apples

Makes 4 servings

1 ½ **cups thinly sliced tart apples**
Juice of 1 lemon
4 **chicken breasts**
¼ **cup flour**
4 **tablespoons butter**
½ **to 1 cup apple cider**
Grated rind of 1 lemon
½ **teaspoon ground ginger**
1 **cup heavy cream**

Sprinkle apples with lemon juice; set aside. Dredge chicken in flour. Heat butter over medium heat in large, heavy skillet. Sauté chicken in butter until both sides are golden.

Add ½ cup cider; cover pan. Cook on low heat for 30 to 40 minutes, or until chicken is tender and juices run clear when pricked with a fork. Add more cider during cooking, if needed to keep chicken from sticking. Remove chicken; place on warm platter and keep warm. Pour drippings into a measuring cup; add cider, if needed to equal ¼ cup. Return liquid to skillet; stir in lemon rind and ginger. Stir in cream; heat on high, stirring constantly until mixture is somewhat reduced and sauce thickens slightly. Stir in apples; heat until apples are just tender and warmed through. Pour over chicken and serve.

Vegetable Fromage

2 **8-ounce packages cream cheese at room temperature**
¼ **cup plain yogurt**
¼ **cup shredded carrot**
¼ **cup finely chopped radish**
¼ **cup finely chopped red pepper**
¼ **cup finely chopped green pepper**
¼ **cup finely sliced green onion or cilantro**
Whole grain breadsticks

Combine all ingredients except breadsticks in blender or food processor just until mixed—do not puree. Use immediately or refrigerate, covered, up to 2 days. Bring to room temperature before serving with whole grain breadsticks.

Braised Celery Almondine

Makes 4 servings

1 **bunch celery**
½ **yellow onion, finely chopped**
¼ **cup coarsely chopped whole almonds**
1 **tablespoon butter**
1 **grated lemon peel**

Separate celery into stalks and wash in hot water; drain. Cut diagonally into ½-inch pieces; add to enough boiling water to cover. Blanch 5 minutes. Drain. Meanwhile, in a large skillet, sauté onion and almonds in butter. Add lemon peel and celery. Toss to coat celery.

Magic

Sometimes I go back to my childhood
And memories my heart seem to fill,
But most of all I remember
The pear trees that grew on the hill.

In springtime they burst into blossom—
White, like mountains of snow.
The air was filled with their fragrance,
And the hill was a magic glow.

Now every year when it's springtime,
I want to go back again;
I wonder if they are still magic
And if the fragrance will be the same.

Laura Hope Marshall

Hills of Home

Sing me a song of windswept hills
Where trees reach up to the sky
And children play on a windy day
As cloud ships sail on high.
Sing me a song of goldenrods
That sway in the gentle breeze
And of cardinals that flit from limb to limb
In stately sycamore trees.

Sing me a song of a lilac lane
That spreads a fragrant shawl,
While roses twine with ivy vine
Along the garden wall.
Sing me a song of a bubbling brook
Where barefoot children play,
Not caring that the coming years
Will steal their youth away.

Sing me a song of windswept hills,
And once again I'll see
The windswept hills of childhood days—
The hills so dear to me.

Juanita Johnson

Grandma's Garden

When lilacs bloom in springtime
And their fragrance fills the air,
Then I journey back to childhood,
To a lovely garden there.

I walk upon a winding path
Between the shrubs and trees
And stop to pick white violets
And watch the honey bees.

Around the bend a bed of blue—
Grape-hyacinths I see,
And lilies-of-the-valley bloom
Beneath the cherry trees.

Clumps of white narcissus
Close by the old pear tree
And rows of dark red peonies
Nod gently in the breeze.

The quince's pale pink blossoms
And the spice bush near the well,
The dear old oxheart cherry tree
From which I nearly fell,

The graceful stems of bleeding hearts,
The pansies' saucy faces,
The feathery ferns in shady nooks,
And spider webs like laces.

Grandma walked among these flowers.
I shall always see her there
When the lilacs bloom in springtime
And their fragrance fills the air.

Doris C. Starr

Photo Opposite
GARDEN GROTTO
Ken Dequaine

Introduction to Spring

There was always that first day of spring. What date the calendar said didn't make any difference. The first day of spring was the morning we came down to breakfast to find the kitchen door open. Released by the last snow, the misty perfume of earth mingled with the wonderful smells of bacon and coffee my mother was creating on the coal oil stove. No more wood stove until fall!

Crowded about the kitchen table covered with white oilcloth, my three brothers and I would make a terrible din until Father came to take his place at the head of the table. Mother filled our mugs with hot cocoa and Father's and hers with steaming black coffee, and then placed two platters in front of Father. There were always two. One held golden strips of crisp bacon or pink slices of ham running little

rivers of goodness into the platter. The other was full to running over with eggs.

When the platters were in place and Mother had taken her seat at the far end of the table, we all bowed our heads and held hands as Father said grace. His "Amen" was a signal to eat but not to talk. Our household was governed by the rule: "Children should be seen and not heard." Father and Mother talked over our heads, discussing plans for the day.

We were eating, but I was also sorting out sounds and watching the spring morning through the open door. A robin swayed, his little throat pulsing with joy, among the bursting buds of the old maple tree. Beneath the tree an old hen, chained to the earth, scratched and clucked to her brood while her husband strutted about pretending to be master of all he surveyed.

When the last bit of bacon had been eaten, each plate cleaned with toast or a hot biscuit, and all the cocoa drained from our mugs, we waited. Finally, when we could wait no longer, Father would say, "You may be excused now," and we could at last burst forth into spring.

Dorothy Muir

Triumph

The plaudits of the populace,
   The palms to pad his path
Our Lord received with humble grace;
   He knew the aftermath.
Yes, "meek and sitting on an ass"
   Their "King" they would behold.
This prophecy had come to pass
   The way it was foretold.

He was embraced with love and trust.
   "Hosannah!" was the cry
That on the morrow so unjust
   Would turn to "Crucify!"
'Twas part and parcel of the plan
   His Father had prepared
Indelibly to leave with man
   As proof of how he cared.

What meant this triumph on the road?
   A saddened Jesus knew
That fame was but an episode
   Oft fickle and untrue;
This thought was left for all who live
   Illumined by this day.
The lasting triumph God would give
   Was still one week away.

Margaret Rorke

And when the hour was come, he sat down, and the twelve apostles with him.

And he said unto them, With desire I have desired to eat this passover with you before I suffer:

For I say unto you, I will not any more eat thereof, until it be fulfilled in the kingdom of God.

And he took the cup, and gave thanks, and said, Take this, and divide it among yourselves:

For I say unto you, I will not drink of the fruit of the vine, until the kingdom of God shall come.

And he took bread, and gave thanks, and brake it, and gave unto them, saying, This is my body which is given for you: this do in remembrance of me.

Likewise also the cup after supper, saying, This cup is the new testament in my blood, which is shed for you.

Luke 22:14-20

And they came to a place which was named Gethsemane: and he saith to his disciples, Sit ye here, while I shall pray.

And he taketh with him Peter and James and John, and began to be sore amazed, and to be very heavy;

And saith unto them, My soul is exceeding sorrowful unto death; tarry ye here and watch.

And he went forward a little, and fell on the ground, and prayed that, if it were possible, the hour might pass from him.

And he said, Abba, Father, all things are possible unto thee; take away this cup from me: nevertheless not what I will, but what thou wilt.

Mark 14:32-36

Gethsemane

There is a way which man hath trod
For lo, these thronging, countless years;
It is the way of life, of God;
It is the way of night, of tears;
Its winding we may not foresee;
It is the way—Gethsemane.

It is the way whereby we know
Life's larger meanings and its claims,
The fellowship of human woe;
Our partnership with others' pains.
It is the way which seems to be
Life's only way—Gethsemane.

Charles Russell Wakeley

And it was the preparation of the passover, and about the sixth hour: and he saith unto the Jews, Behold your King!

But they cried out, Away with him, away with him, crucify him. Pilate saith unto them, Shall I crucify your King? The chief priests answered, We have no king but Caesar.

Then delivered he him therefore unto them to be crucified. And they took Jesus, and led him away.

And he bearing his cross went forth into a place called the place of a skull, which is called in the Hebrew Golgotha:

Where they crucified him, and two other with him, on either side one, and Jesus in the midst.

And Pilate wrote a title, and put it on the cross. And the writing was, JESUS OF NAZARETH THE KING OF THE JEWS.

This title then read many of the Jews: for the place where Jesus was crucified was nigh to the city: and it was written in Hebrew, and Greek, and Latin.

Then said the chief priests of the Jews to Pilate, Write not, The King of the Jews; but that he said, I am King of the Jews.

Pilate answered, What I have written I have written.

John 19:14-22

In the end of the sabbath, as it began to dawn toward the first day of the week, came Mary Magdalene and the other Mary to see the sepulchre.

And, behold, there was a great earthquake: for the angel of the Lord descended from heaven, and came and rolled back the stone from the door, and sat upon it.

His countenance was like lightning, and his raiment white as snow:

And for fear of him the keepers did shake, and became as dead men.

And the angel answered and said unto the women, Fear not ye: for I know that ye seek Jesus, which was crucified.

He is not here: for he is risen, as he said. Come, see the place where the Lord lay.

And go quickly, and tell his disciples that he is risen from the dead; and behold, he goeth before you into Galilee; there shall ye see him: lo, I have told you.

And they departed quickly from the sepulchre with fear and great joy; and did run to bring his disciples word.

Matthew 28:1-8

The Promise of Easter

The stone is rolled away;
Behold the empty tomb!
The Resurrection dawn
Dispels earth's deepest gloom.

Victorious over death;
He rose to bless mankind
With radiant hope and faith
In glory undefined.

Anew the promise comes
With all the joy it brings;
Across the centuries
The Easter message rings.

Edith Shaw Butler

courtesy of *American Agriculturist*

Photo Opposite
THE LORD IS RISEN
H. Armstrong Roberts

Hope

There's power in the towering hills
And harmony in a tree.
There's music in a flowing stream
And legions in the sea.

There's wonder in the twinkling stars
And magic in the moon.
There's hidden lore in desert lands
And mystery in lagoons.

There's peace encased in gardens
And food in fields of grain.
There's fragrance in the regal rose
And health in snow and rain.

There's music in the treetops,
And birdsongs fill the air.
A soothing touch in Mother's hand,
And comfort in Father's prayer.

There's sacredness in God's great plan
And his last Gethsemane.
For victory rode his darkest hour
With hope for you and me.

Mamie Ozburn Odum

$\mathfrak{I}$ will lift up mine eyes unto the hills, from whence cometh my help.

My help cometh from the Lord, which made heaven and earth.

He will not suffer thy foot to be moved: he that keepeth thee will not slumber.

Behold, he that keepeth Israel shall neither slumber nor sleep.

The Lord is that keeper: the Lord is thy shade upon thy right hand.

The sun shall not smite thee by day, nor the moon by night.

The Lord shall preserve thee from all evil: he shall preserve thy soul.

The Lord shall preserve thy going out and thy coming in from this time forth, and even for evermore.

Psalm 121

Pine Bough Chapel

My chapel is an orchard,
My aisle the golden grain,
My stained glass windows tinged
   with blue
Over all the meadows reign.

My pew is cushioned clover,
My wine the morning dew,
The hymnals carved by
   windsong pen
And etched in rainbow hue.

The robin is my church bell,
The violets my bouquet,
As the reverend clothed in
   fragrant robe
Arrives by pine bough sleigh.

Gail L. Roberson

Garden in Spring

My garden woke at dawn's first
   light.
Spring touched each growing
   thing last night;

The tulips wore new bonnets
   gay,
The dogwood stood in white
   array,
The weeping willow trailed new
   green
Into the pond's bright mirror
   sheen,
Bobwhite called from the lilac
   tree,
Each daffodil cupped a honey
   bee.

And I, in awesome wonder stood
To view the handiwork of God.

Carol Bessent Hayman

Easter Yesterdays

As Eastertime rolls 'round again
   we think of yesterday,
Perhaps because of many things
   that Easter brought our way.

Things were different way back then
   in styles and dress and age,
And Easter was a childhood joy
   of bunnies, chicks, and eggs.

So today, nostalgic memories
   aslip back into the years
As we remember Mother
   and the Easters she made dear.

She looked at fashion pictures
   then sewed and made our dresses.
Indeed all new spring outfits
   were her handcrafted best.

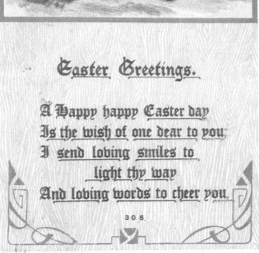

Easter Greetings.

A Happy happy Easter day
Is the wish of one dear to you;
I send loving smiles to
light thy way
And loving words to cheer you.

305

But then she told us Easter Day
   was not for clothes alone;
It was a time for church and prayer
   and rejoicing, too, at home.

It seemed a bit like Christmas,
   with the family home and all.
With Easter eggs and baskets
   there was joy for one and all.

And, alikened unto Christmas Eve,
   we awaited Easter morn;
And just as like that Christmas Day,
   Christ again was born.

In our sleepy little neighborhood
   the church bells rang anew,
And folks rejoiced in grateful prayer
   just as today we do.

And when one is in the sunshine
   of youth and reveries,
Today the past, though vanished,
   contains cheerful memories.

                Edith M. Helstern

EASTER CARDS by Al Riccio
EASTER EGG COLLECTION by Joanne Kash from the collection of Sue Lofaro

A Remembrance of Easter

Happy Easter...what a day it was
When we were young;
First, to church, to sing and pray,
Then later came the fun.
In secret places Mom had hidden
Colored eggs for us to find,
While festive cookies, hot cross buns
Were constantly on our minds.
All week long, Mom had cooked and baked
Before the big day came.
Pa chopped wood, the yard was raked,
And everyone pitched in.
When at last we took our place
With friends and family
And Grandpa said the usual grace,
We feasted handsomely.
Then on our separate ways we'd go
And from our baskets eat
Jelly beans, and nibble slow
The chocolate bunny treat.

Elsie Natalie Brady

I Wonder

Do you suppose, in Bunny Town,
There is a little shop
Where rabbits like to buy their clothes
When they go for a hop?
Do they find hats to fit their ears
And neckties, blossom pink?
What will they spend for fancy gloves
Or slippers, do you think?

I wonder if they stop to chat
Down in the woodland glade
And will they have on Easter morn
A holiday parade?
Will someone think to peddle joy,
As Easter bunnies do,
And leave some eggs beside their door?
I'm wondering, aren't you?

Marguerite Gode

Photo Opposite
A CLUSTER OF BUNNIES
Barry L. Runk
Grant Heilman Photography

Easter Morning

Frisky little Easter bunnies
In jackets bright and gay
Are laden with their woven baskets
This bright and happy day.

Dashing swiftly to and fro
From bushes, stumps, and trees,
Hiding colorful Easter eggs
So nary a child can see.

One behind the peony bush
And one near the red brick wall,
Another by the wishing well
Till they're hidden one and all.

Laughing children soon appear
With faces beaming bright,
Scanning quickly here and there
For baskets out of sight.

Skipping wildly through the yard,
Searching near the ground;
Scrambling to each hiding place
Till every basket's found!

Ruth H. Underhill

April

They call their baby "April."
Oh, what a lovely name!
It conjures up a picture
Too free to fit a frame:

A dainty little blossom—
A tiny crocus bud—
That pushes past dissuasion
To part the melting mud;

A timid, furry bunny,
A yellow-feathered chick,
A glimpse of green transfusing
What had appeared a stick;

A robin brightly breasted
A-singing to the sky
As if to ask for color
To use for eggshell dye;

A branch of pussy willow,
A brook with babbling tongue,
A lambkin in a meadow:
Just all that's fresh and young.

They call their baby "April"—
The month of hope and cheer.
How nice to carry "April"
Around with one all year!

Margaret Rorke

The Little Sailor Girl

I saw her walking down the hill
In her Easter outfit new;
She toddled toward the old church door,
This lass of not quite two.

She wore a little sailor coat
Tied with a bow of red,
And a perky little sailor hat
Was perched upon her head.

I wanted so to hold her close,
This little sailor girl,
But with her eyes she said to me,
"Don't touch; you'll muss a curl."

Intrigued, I watched her climb the steps
And shake the preacher's hand;
Then down the aisle she briskly walked
At her mother's command.

Quite silently she took her place
In the quaint, old-fashioned pew;
She sang and dropped her penny
When the offering plate passed through.

I'm sure that Jesus smiled upon
His child in outfit new,
As to his house she came that morn
In red and white and blue.

Loise Pinkerton Fritz

Photo Overleaf
ANTELOPE BUTTE RESERVE
Ed Cooper

THE
MONDAY
AFTER

Green snatches of
    shredded cellophane grass
lie in sparse patches
    on my family room rug.

Baskets now boasting only
    jelly beans and candy wrappers
sit dejectedly atop my
    finger-smudged coffee table.

A decapitated chocolate bunny
    lies melting in
        reluctant April sun.

Somehow the color and pageantry of Easter
    seem so much further away
        than only yesterday.

As I reach for the melting mess,
    a mass of lavender
        rolls from behind the drape—
a forgotten Easter egg.

Its shell is finely cracked;
    tiny lines crisscross its surface
        like winding roads on a pastel map.

This one egg
    eluded the children
in the frenzied flurry
    of hiding and finding.

I stand over the kitchen sink
        to peel my purple egg,
    watch shattered shell fall away
        to reveal a flawless surface
            of pearly white.

I place it on a plate and,
    armed with salt and pepper,
prepare to make a meal
    of this egg-hunt fugitive.

But first I bow my head
    to offer thanks for
        lost things found,
            inner beauty,

and for this
battered bit of Easter
    come to color my Monday
        with just a touch of wonder.

Mary Lou Carney

Nature's Creed

I believe in the brook as it wanders
From hillside into glade;
I believe in the breeze as it whispers
When evening's shadows fade.
I believe in the roar of the river
As it dashes from high cascade;
I believe in the cry of the tempest
'Mid the thunder's cannonade.
I believe in the light of shining stars;
I believe in the sun and the moon.
I believe in the flash of lightning;
I believe in the night bird's croon.
I believe in the faith of the flowers,
I believe in the rock and sod;
For in all of these appeareth clear
The handiwork of God.

Anonymous

Photo Opposite
SPRING STREAM
Ed Cooper

Country Chronicle

An Easter chorale resounds through hill and valley with each returning spring. The cantata begins, a symbol of renewal and resurrection. The season never fails to free the land of the shackles of winter. The soil stirs with seed and sprout. Our faith is strengthened by an everlasting continuity from season to season, from year to year, through time without end.

Easter is as alive and vibrant as the springtime which surrounds it. It prepares the way to green pastures and paths by still waters. Easter inspires; it is as comforting and consoling as the first birdsongs of spring. There is an assurance of eternal life; the miracle of resurrection is evident everywhere. There is a reawakening in our own being and in the natural world around us. As the earth's bounty returns to bloom, a country dweller's pulse quickens, flowing as freely as an upland stream in March and April.

Listen to the music that pours from every nook and corner of the countryside. The vernal equinox has set the stage for the festival of Easter, celebrating the glorious resurrection of Christ. Hymns of praise and joy issue from tree and thicket, from meadow, marsh, and wood.

The days of spring are filled with song. Listen to the birds as they sing the morning processional. Robins carol the vespers in the backyard elms in late afternoon; and when April's peepers pipe from marsh and bog, the clear bell-like chorus becomes the recessional—those hours when the night's cloak of darkness hovers over the land until the dawn of tomorrow's sun.

Lansing Christman

Miracle of Spring

Cold March winds blow and there is snow,
But April will bring showers.
White fields will turn to shades of green
And flourish with bright flowers.

Leaf buds will cover barren trees,
Birds will return and sing,
Small seeds will grow—I do believe
In miracles of spring.

Esther F. Thom

Entwined

Spring
wraps itself around me like a vine
till body, mind, and soul
are well entwined.

Awakened
like the earth, I am renewed,
aroused
by nature's stirring interlude.

Leigh Cheney

The Daffodils

I wandered lonely as a cloud
That floats on high o'er vales and hills,
When all at once I saw a crowd,
A host of golden daffodils,
Beside the lake, beneath the trees
Fluttering and dancing in the breeze.

Continuous as the stars that shine
And twinkle on the Milky Way,
They stretched in never-ending line
Along the margin of a bay;
Ten thousand saw I at a glance
Tossing their heads in sprightly dance.

The waves beside them danced, but they
Outdid the sparkling waves in glee:
A poet could not but be gay
In such a jocund company!
I gazed—and gazed—but little thought
What wealth the show to me had brought:

For oft, when on my couch I lie
In vacant or in pensive mood,
They flash upon that inward eye
Which is the bliss of solitude;
And then my heart with pleasure fills,
And dances with the daffodils.

William Wordsworth

Spring Flowers

Spring flowers always come as a surprise,
   A blessed treat for winter-weary eyes.
We had forgotten just how fresh and bright
   A daffodil could be and how the light
Seemed to be 'prisoned in the tulip's cup
   Like tiny empty goblets lifted up.

A purple crocus on its furry stalk
   Peeps through the new clean grass beside the walk.
Lupins in their gay attire look
   Like little people from a storybook,
Tripping along to join a spring parade,
   Decked in their feast day costumes quaintly made.

A primrose never seems one half so fair
   As when we find a fresh one growing where
All winter long a bank of snow has lain.
   And daisies bordering a field of grain,
Fall wheat, or barley green as Irish grass
   Give a pledge of summer as we pass.

Strange how a slender stalk of columbine
   Can send small quivers up and down your spine.
Pansies that blush at their own loveliness
   Lift their little faces up to us...
No wonder flowers come as a surprise,
   Bringing the light to winter-weary eyes.

Edna Jaques

Photo Opposite
PANSIES
Fred Sieb

These Moments

April has kept its promise
To return again this year,
Bringing the kiss of springtime
With its blessings of good cheer.

The pitter-patter of raindrops
Awakes the sleeping flowers;
The robin lends his music
Through all his waking hours.

Perfume is wafting gently
On wings of a springtime breeze;
I'm grateful to the Father
For moments such as these.

These moments of transition
From wintry winds to spring—
These moments make me happy
And cause my heart to sing!

Georgia B. Adams

Boughs of Spring

A song of spring is in the air—
A promise to behold.
Curling tendrils seek the sun;
Green boughs of spring unfold.

And in my heart that song of spring
Is in each bough of green,
For God is in the heart that sings
And seeks tomorrow's dream.

There's promise in each bursting bud
With blossoms yet to be,
Lifting petals one by one
In springtime rhapsody.

The world awakes refreshed anew,
Again remembering
That sweet rebirth returns to earth
With greening boughs of spring.

Mildred L. Jarrell

Photo Overleaf
TROUT LAKE
Ed Cooper

Forest Meditations

If I'm out walking by myself,
please do not follow me;
I seek the silent forest
with her fragrant green and growing trees.

Pray, don't disturb my wanderings
nor glimpse my naked soul,
as I pull back the curtain
for the author of this mortal scroll.

This time is mine to revel in,
to share with God alone;
so please continue on your way,
assured that I will soon be home.

Leigh Cheney

Vagabond

Today I decided to wander away
Beyond the pasture gate,
Follow the winding river
Where the weeping willows wait.

I talked to the redwing blackbird
As he fashioned his house of twigs,
Spent a moment in contemplation
Of some pussy willow sprigs.

Then off on the trail of a bluebird
To a stump beyond the hill,
Where I dozed in the warm spring sunshine
To the tune of the woodthrush trill.

Pauline Mulford

In Praise of Mothers

Which memory of your mother is your favorite? Was it that special dessert she made for your birthday? Or the way her caring and soothing touch always eased any hurt—even the emotional ones? Was it the helpful advice given to an insecure teenager? Or how about...?

In our next issue, *Mother's Day Ideals,* we honor all mothers as we celebrate their beautiful day in May. Join us as we share this special occasion with readers like Mildred R. Robins of Salt Lake City, Utah, who writes:

> In all of the years that I have been a subscriber, each issue that arrives is like opening up a very special gift! I am enthralled anew every time! Thank you for publishing such a beautiful and wholesome publication.

We also appreciate the words of Mrs. B.R. Clark of Portland, Oregon, who writes:

> You publish one of the most beautiful magazines I have ever had the pleasure of reading. The articles are so inspiring and bring wonderful memories to everyone who reads them. I can almost live every story and poem.... Keep up the good work.

Thank you, Mrs. Robins and Mrs. Clark! Sharing *Ideals* with you is an honor. We hope our other readers will help us share *Ideals* with their friends by starting a gift subscription with *Mother's Day.*

ACKNOWLEDGMENTS

THE MONDAY AFTER by Mary Lou Carney from her book *A MONTH OF MONDAYS,* copyright © 1984 by Abingdon Press. Used by permission; GARDEN IN SPRING by Carol Bessent Hayman, published in *VISTA 1978* and *MATURE LIVING 1985;* MARCH SNOW by Garnett Ann Schultz from her book *SOMETHING BEAUTIFUL,* copyright © 1966; GETHSEMANE by Charles Russell Wakeley from *1000 QUOTABLE POEMS—VOL. 1,* copyright 1928 by Willett, Clark & Colby, compiled by Thomas Curtis Clark. Our sincere thanks to the following whose addresses we were unable to locate: Christel B. Ellis for A BOY AND SPRINGTIME; Marguerite Gode for I WONDER; Dorothy Muir for INTRODUCTION TO SPRING: Doris C. Starr for GRANDMA'S GARDEN.